Pet Corner

W9-ADB-361

PLAYFUL PARAKEETS

By Katie Kawa

 **Gareth Stevens**
Publishing

Please visit our website, www.garethstevens.com. For a free color catalog of all our high-quality books, call toll free 1-800-542-2595 or fax 1-877-542-2596.

Library of Congress Cataloging-in-Publication Data

Kawa, Katie.
Playful parakeets / Katie Kawa.
    p. cm. — (Pet corner)
ISBN 978-1-4339-5611-9 (pbk.)
ISBN 978-1-4339-5612-6 (6-pack)
ISBN 978-1-4339-5609-6 (library binding)
1. Parrots—Juvenile literature. I. Title.
SF473.P3K39 2011
636.6'865—dc22

                                2010053825

First Edition

Published in 2012 by
Gareth Stevens Publishing
111 East 14th Street, Suite 349
New York, NY 10003

Copyright © 2012 Gareth Stevens Publishing

Editor: Katie Kawa
Designer: Andrea Davison-Bartolotta

Photo credits: Cover, p. 15 iStockphoto/Thinkstock; p. 1 Jupiterimages/Photos.com/Thinkstock; pp. 5, 7, 9, 11, 17, 21, 23, 24 (all) Shutterstock.com; p. 13 Julie Toy/Taxi/Getty Images; p. 19 Frank Greenaway/Dorling Kindersley/ Getty Images.

Printed in the United States of America

CPSIA compliance information: Batch #CS11GS: For further information contact Gareth Stevens, New York, New York at 1-800-542-2595.

Contents

A parakeet is a kind of bird. Parakeets are smart!

Parakeets can talk!

7

Parakeets learn tricks. They learn to sit on people's fingers!

A parakeet has a long tail.

A parakeet lives in a big cage. It needs room to move.

13

The cage is cleaned every week. New paper goes in the cage.

Parakeets fly outside of their cage. This is their exercise.

Parakeets love water. They take baths to stay clean.

Parakeets break seeds open. This is how they eat.

Parakeets sleep standing up.

Words to Know

fingers

seeds

tail

Index